£2

COMMON SENSE ABOUT YOGA

Swami Pavitrananda

Advaita Ashrama
(Publication Department)
5 Dehi Entally Road
Kolkata 700 014

Published by
Swami Bodhasarananda
President, Advaita Ashrama
Mayavati, Champawat, Uttarakhand
from its Publication Department, Kolkata
Email : mail@advaitaashrama.org
Website : www.advaitaashrama.org

Sixteenth Impression, May 2007
3M3C

ISBN 81-7505-048-9

Printed in India at
Trio Process
Kolkata 700 014

"Anything that is secret and mysterious in these systems of Yoga should be at once rejected. The best guide in life is strength. In religion as in all other matters, discard everything that weakens you, have nothing to do with it. Mystery-mongering weakens the human brain. It has well-nigh destroyed Yoga —one of the grandest of sciences."

SWAMI VIVEKANANDA

PREFACE

These pages have been the outcome of a form of thinking aloud on the subject of Yoga. The language used is not, therefore, of a philosophical treatise.

It is with some hesitation that these unvarnished thoughts are sent out in print—in the hope that there might be a fellow-traveller in the path or a co-aspirant after the goal.

So much has been said and written about Yoga—some of it with undisputed authority by a spiritual giant like Swami Vivekananda—that this little book cannot claim to say anything new or original on the subject. As its prosaic title implies, its main object is to discuss the science of Yoga in as simple and rational a manner as possible; and also to debunk some of the nonsense that continues to be said and believed on the subject.

THE AUTHOR

MAYAVATI, HIMALAYAS
1944

CONTENTS

CONTENTS

THE MYSTERIES OF YOGA

From very ancient times the general mass of the people in all countries has associated religion with mysteries, miracles, and supernatural phenomena. In early days people believed that evil spirits were the cause of all diseases, and priests were often summoned to exorcise the Devil. Even today there are persons everywhere who will seek the help of priests, Sannyasins, or Yogis for the cure of physical ailments. This practice is common not only among the ignorant, but extends to the educated classes. Even rationalists and those who are proud of their practical wisdom sometimes fall back on supernatural remedies, as a last resort, when all other efforts have failed. There is also a tendency, especially among the rich, to seek the advice of those professing religion on short-cuts to worldly success. Many of them visit Sadhus simply for the purpose of knowing, if possible, what further material rewards the future holds for them: to them, Religion and Astrology mean the same thing! In the West a large number of persons who are ignorant of the real conditions in India still think of Hinduism in terms of Astrology or Palmistry: for them every Indian they meet in a train or on board a ship is a potential fortune-teller!

Is it then a matter for any wonder if there are adventurers, everywhere, ready to take advantage of this "mystery-mongering" propensity of the majority of men and women? In almost every country these charlatans ply a flourishing trade in the name of Religion. There is the story of the "Swami" in a large American city who, among his various Courses of Instruction, advertised also: "Course of ten lessons for the attainment of Nirvana—Ten Dollars"! When upbraided by a fellow Indian for practising such a hoax, the "Swami" tried to justify his action by saying that, after a long and fruitless search for an honest job, he had at last hit upon this device because he saw no harm in trading on the credulity of fools!

Deception of this kind has gone to the farthest limit in the case of Yoga—that much abused aspect of Hindu Mysticism. People have all sorts of queer ideas about Yoga. Not long ago a pompous-looking individual, calling himself Professor of Yoga, delivered a lecture before a respectable gathering in a leading city of India, during which he described Yoga as mainly the method of acquiring miraculous powers over the body. He illustrated his theme by the usual drinking of sulphuric acid, munching of glass and swallowing of fire, among other "miracles". The real *miracle,* however, was that, during the discussion which followed the "learned" lecture, no one in the audience which contained persons from all walks of life, had the thought of asking the "fire-eating" professor what bearing all his talk and "bag of tricks" had on the spiritual life!

Some persons go to the Himalayas in search of Yogis and Mahatmas, and come back terribly disappointed if they could not meet even one who performed miracles. A few of these miracle-hunters, after repeated failures, turn bitter, and try to make dupes of others by writing sensational books on the "secrets" of Yoga, the "hidden abodes" of the Himalayas, and the like.

Being connected with an Ashrama in the Himalayas, the writer has had personal experience—at times amusing, and at times very sad—of what strange ideas people sometimes have regarding Yogis and imaginary Mahatmas supposed to be living in those mountains. Not long ago an American wrote to ask if he could come to the Himalayas to practise Yoga. He was apparently disappointed when he received the reply that he could as well practise Yoga at home provided he developed faith in and devotion to God. This is a typical instance of an unfortunate attitude of mind which shows how uncommon is "common sense" in religious matters. It may happen that sometimes a person in search of a miracle-worker deserves sympathy on account of some sudden calamity that has weakened his reasoning power; but there are others who seem deliberately to relinquish all claim to reason as soon as they speak of religion.

Those who have lived in the Himalayas for a long time, and are honest, will admit that the mere proximity of those lofty mountains is not sufficient for the attainment of Yoga. No doubt the environment of the Himalayas offers many great advantages, but that alone is no guarantee for one's spiritual success in life. Even in the remotest corners of the Himalayas there are persons who live the same kind of life as those in the plains. The solitude and sublimity of the high snows has no spiritual value for them. By seeking the recesses of the Himalayas one may get temporary peace or respite from the troubles of life, but the vagaries of the mind soon return and continue their old game. It is only by ceaseless struggle that one gets strength, and it is by dint of hard labour alone that success in spiritual life is achieved by the strong. Only a very few, however, are prepared to pay the heavy price demanded for such achievement: the rest are content to run after cheap and tawdry remedies or to waste their time in the search of occult methods and secret places.

What, then, is Yoga? What does it connote and what does it aim at? Yoga literally means "connection" or "union" Philosophically, it means union with the Supreme Spirit. What unites us with the Supreme Spirit is Yoga. There is only "one" in the universe: when seen through the prism of ignorance, It appears to be many. Because of ignorance we feel ourselves separate from the Supreme Self, and from one another, and see an endless variety of things without their underlying unity. Here arises the trouble. Wherever there are two, or more than two, there is the cause of fear, jealousy, hatred, competition, and consequently of human misery. When there is only one, who will fear whom, who will hate whom? All that we see in the universe is I, and I alone. I cannot even think, because the thinker and the thought are one and the same. When that state is attained, all human misery disappears.

Technically, the word "Yoga" has been used to refer to the system of philosophy propounded by the Sage Patanjali, about the second century B. C. But, in general, Yoga may be called a method by which one can remove "ignorance", the cause of manifoldness, and thus attain union with the Supreme Self. Though there is only One existence in the absolute sense, it is nevertheless a fact—as hard a fact as a piece of stone which we touch—that there is manifoldness in the universe. However much we may philosophise about the one universal Existence, in actual life we suffer when our relations die, when we get disease or meet with disappointments. Sometimes even the trifle of an angry word, which has no more significance than a puff of wind, upsets our balance of mind to such a degree that we suffer for days and months together. No amount of philosophy can remove this suffering unless it is accompanied by practice based on the experience of those who have *found* Ultimate Reality or the Supreme Self. Yoga, therefore, accepts the life situation as we find it, and suggests methods by which we can transcend human limitations.

The dominant factors in our lives are feeling, thought, and action, the mind being the motivating force behind all. Because there is the feeling factor, we feel misery and run after pleasure. If we could control our feelings and emotions and give them the right direction, we would seek real happiness instead of sense pleasure, and thus attain that Joy "which passeth all understanding".

The method by which we can attain such Joy by turning all our emotions towards the Supreme Reality—in other words, attain union with God through devotion—is called Bhakti-Yoga. The method of discrimination by which we can realise our identify with the Ultimate Existence is called Jnana-Yoga or the Science of Wisdom. The art of detachment by which we can govern all our activities so that we may not be entangled in the meshes of work, though we are engaged in it, is called Karma-Yoga or the Science of Work. Finally, the method by which we can control the mind itself, which is the cause of all our misery, is called Raja-Yoga.

It will thus be seen that there is no more "mystery" in Yoga than what is embedded in the very existence of the Universe. It will also be found that the art and science of Yoga are processes which are intrinsically simple, clear, and straightforward; although success in their application can be achieved only by hard labour, ceaseless struggle, and vigilant care. Persons with ulterior motives may make use of Yoga for unworthy purposes; but those who are genuine aspirants after the goal of union with the Ultimate Reality, or Freedom from bondage, will go straight for the mark, and not tarry on the way, lured by diversions like the hunt for supernatural phenomena or powers.

BHAKTI-YOGA

"Bhakti" means intense love of God and Bhakti-Yoga is the path by which God may be realised through love and devotion. Now the questions are: What is the nature of God? What is the proof that God exists? Without knowing the answer to these questions one cannot expect to have love for God. From time immemorial there had been a class of people in this world with whom the problem was not whether God exists, but how to realise Him. That God does exist was an axiomatic truth with them from their very early age; their struggle was only how to intensify their devotion so that He might be realised as a fact. They did not start life with philosophical questionings; philosophical systems were built on what they said and experienced *after* they had attained the spiritual summum bonum. They went straight to the spiritual path, and when they had reached the end and the goal, they served as beacon lights to humanity. Such were the prophets and the saints who afterwards became the spiritual and moral teachers of the world. Some of these great souls had not known even the rudiments of learning; but, propelled by an inner urge of spiritual hankering, they had sought and achieved the Great Unknown.

Christ said, "Ask, and it shall be given you; seek, and ye shall find." Yes, he and others of his class sought and sought so intensely that the great mystery of the Universe was unravelled before them.

Kabir, the great medieval saint of India, said with regard to spiritual pursuits:

मोको कहाँ तू ढूंढ़े बन्दे मैं तो तेरे पास में।
खोंजोगे तो अभी मिलूंगा, पल भर की तलाश में॥

"Where dost thou seek Me? I am just by your side. If you sincerely seek Me, I will be got in one moment."

Sri Ramakrishna used to say:

"If one can have the same intensity of love for God as the combined love of the miser for his money, the mother for her son and the lover foı the beloved, one can very easily realise Him. But who has that? One will shed a jugful of tears for earthly relations, but who will weep for God?"

Mohammed said:

"If you walk to God, God will run to you!"

Francis Thompson, the Catholic poet, expressed a similar sentiment when he sang of

God as *The Hound of Heaven*:

"I fled Him, down the nights and down the days;
I fled Him, down the arches of the years;
I fled Him, down the labyrinthine ways
Of my own mind; and in the mist of tears
I hid from Him, and under running laughter.

.. ..

But with unhurrying chase,
And unperturbed pace,
Deliberate speed, majestic instancy,
They beat... ."

Those strong Feet of God follow the fugitive until he is at last caught by Divine Love.

Those indeed are fortunate who, because of their innate and childlike love for God, either turn to Him as naturally as a duckling takes to water, or are sought by him and taken into His Arms. But what about those who, although perfectly sincere, have not that early and spontaneous love for God; and who are assailed by a thousand and one doubts not only whether God actually exists, but even whether it is worth while aspiring after God when innumerable sense objects offer one the immediate prospect of pleasure and enjoyment? Between the natural lovers of God at one extreme and rank materialists at the other, there come a large number of persons who walk halfway between light and darkness, who have a good deal of spiritual hankering but who cannot rise above the temptations of the world. Their lot is very miserable indeed because of the conflict in their souls. While the path of Discrimination or Jnana-Yoga, may attract the unbending realist, the person whose heart is sadly torn between the world of flesh and the world of the Spirit, may often find peace and illumination by following the path of Love or Bhakti-Yoga. It is for such persons that every religion prescribes different forms of prayers and rituals, different methods of spiritual practices. Ritualism is a kind of Kindergarten for spiritual novices and consists mainly of the worship of God in various forms and the reading of scriptures containing the sayings of prophets and saints. For the majority of spiritual aspirants the path of spiritual life is long and tortuous, the goal distant and dim. But those who are sincere and endure till the end, generally achieve success, because God judges the devotee not by the amount of spiritual labour that he has undergone but by the intensity of his struggle. In spiritual life, it sometimes happens that when the goal seems to be very, very far away, God is just round the corner, eagerly waiting to reveal Himself to His zealous seeker!

The first step to Bhakti, as universally acknowledged, is prayer. Every religion says that in order to create genuine devotion for God, one has to pray. But a doubting mind will say: "Why should I pray? How can I pray when I have neither seen nor known God? And what is the guarantee that my prayer will ever be heard and answered?" It is, no doubt, true that it is difficult to pray without knowing God; but it is equally true that, without prayer or intense longing, one cannot really know God. At first sight, this may sound paradoxical; but all controversy is set at rest if the doubter can bring himself to believe the testimony of all great prophets and seers that God *does* answer prayer, that no sincere and unselfish prayer ever goes in vain. We cannot ignore the experience of earnest seekers who have realised Truth. If we find it difficult to believe the words of those who lived in the hoary past, there can surely be found persons even in our own times who bear direct testimony to the efficacy of prayer. The day-to-day life of such a person is so full of peace, cheer and unselfish love that it is impossible for any honest person to disbelieve his testimony. Fortunate are these doubters who meet and recognise such persons in early life!

Prayer, in its widest sense, has got a meaning and value even for the philosopher. Although the existence of God as a Supreme Being may be questioned, almost all systems of philosophy recognise the operation in human beings of an inner force of infinite power—for instance, the "elan vital" of Bergson. By intense longing, or prayer, one gets in touch with this infinite power, and then some result inevitably follows. What one may accept, philosophically, as existing within and behind every being in the universe, a devotee sees, emotionally, as an objective power—outside and above him. The Bhakta finds it easier and more joyful to adopt that attitude, because it satisfies his feeling of Love; and it must be recognised that, for a certain type of persons, the demands of the heart are much stronger than those of the intellect.

Some may criticise the Bhakta's attitude on the ground that his conception of God is that of a glorified human being. But a little unbiased reflection would make these critics realise that if a cow could speak, it would say that God was like a cow; or that if a triangle could think, its concept of God would be a vast triangle. The critic cannot disprove the existence of God by merely saying that the human conception of the Supreme Being is purely anthropomorphic. With our limited intellects we cannot conceive of the Infinite: we naturally think of God in terms of our finite minds. A pot or a jar cannot contain all the waters of a sea, but only as much as its capacity. Take a party of travellers consisting of a historian, an archaeologist, a botanist, a geologist, an artist, and a child: when they reach their destination, each will see the place from his own point of view. The historian will search for the spot of historical importance; the archaeologist will run after old buildings or ruins; the botanist will be interested in trees and plants; the geologist will be thinking of the age of the land; the artist will try to reproduce the colours and lines of the surroundings; and perhaps the child will be looking with wonder at the cars and people on the road or at the attractive display of things in a shop window. In the same way our conception of God will vary according to the viewpoint and mental capacity of each one of us; but that does not matter as long as one's genuine spiritual craving is satisfied. In the very nature of things the Infinite is beyond the reach of our finite thought and speech.

To give concrete help to spiritual aspirants of the devotional type of mind, Hinduism has advocated the worship of God in images. This has come in for a good deal of fanatical criticism from those who have not the patience nor the sympathy required for a study of the idea behind all kinds of image worship. Even when a philosopher tries to think of the Infinite, he has to fall back on the conception of some vastness that has come within his experience—a wide space, long stretches of water in the ocean or the great blue sky above. In the last analysis that is also a form of idolatry! In the same way an image is a symbol which helps the devotee to think of God. Just as beautiful scenery often inspires an artist to think of the Great Creator, so a beautiful image is a medium through which a devotee sees his God. Even a child knows that a lump of earth is not God; but that lump when formed into an image may invoke in a devotee's heart the feeling of love for God. Then his mind transcends the earthly materials of the image, and may even ascend to the superconscious state. After all, who can think of the Infinite without the help of some kind of symbol? Those who decry image worship are often found to associate one or other concrete thing with their forms of prayer—a cross, a book, a sacred spot.

Besides prayer and worship, association with advanced souls is also of great value in the development of Bhakti. It is said that even a moment's association with a holy person serves as a boat in which the ocean of the world can be safely crossed. If any one has the good fortune to know a true saint, he gets a glimpse of the Ideal realised in life and is often impelled to seek such a realisation himself. Many persons refuse to believe in the help that can be received from a Guru, or spiritual teacher. According to them there is no necessity for an intermediary in religious life because light can come direct from the Source of all light. This view may be partially the result of the reaction caused by the discovery of many false Gurus who have often made a trade of religion. But barring such exceptions, there is as much necessity of a genuine teacher in the sphere of religion as in other walks of life. Although theoretically a person can have education without a teacher, almost all send their children to schools and colleges. Similarly, it is no doubt possible to realise God without any help from outside, but such a possibility will only be within the capacity of a very rare and exceptional soul. All others must depend on help from more advanced souls. Fortunate, indeed, is the Bhakta who comes across a Guru who is a man of realisation or a highly advanced soul: for such a Guru not only instructs, but is able to transmit to his disciple the strength and power necessary to carry out the instructions. The words of such a spiritual teacher carry a conviction which cannot be got by any other means; and the disciple no longer gropes in darkness but follows a clear path, however difficult. Once contact has been made with a genuine spiritual teacher, the aspirant's progress to the goal is assured. Not that he will not have any further struggle to attain the goal, but that struggle will be minimised a hundredfold. After having met the real teacher, the Bhakta's doubts and vacillation about the path and the goal will vanish and his only concern will be to tread the path, however hard, and to reach the goal. This is not a small matter. While other aspirants are at sea without a rudder or compass, the fortunate disciple has got an experienced pilot to steer his ship and carry it safely ashore. Notwithstanding all this, even the aspirant whose search for a genuine Guru has been temporarily unsuccessful need not despair. If he is sincere, help is bound to come, probably when least expected, as it actually came in the past in many such cases. One thing is certain: the Bhakta who has an earnest hankering for God will make speedier progress, in spite of all handicaps, than the lukewarm aspirant with the best of opportunities.

Most religions prescribe Japa, or the repetition of some sacred words denoting the Godhead, as a preliminary step, like prayer, for the spiritual aspirant. The repetition of the name of God brings into the mind an association of God's attributes and has an uplifting effect. Although association with a genuinely holy person may not always be possible, any one may get at least some of the advantages to be obtained from such association, through the repetition of sacred words. The mind is very hard to control: it wanders, and the more one tries to check it, the more it goes astray. Japa is a quasi-mechanical process of controlling the mind. Saints who actually tried this method have testified how by its use the mind calms down automatically. Thus Dadu, a great saint of India, says:

दादू बिन अवलंबन क्युं रहै मन चंचल चलि जाइ।
अस्थिर मनवां तौ रहै सुमिरण सेती लाइ॥

"How can the mind remain without an object as its support? It will naturally wander hither and thither restlessly. Let the wandering mind constantly remember God, and it will calm down."

Referring to the fact that many take the help of a rosary to make Japa, he says: "Your mind is the rosary which is threaded by the incoming and outgoing breaths. Without having any other rosary in your hands, repeat the name of God in rhythm with your breath. By this process you will realise Brahman."

Tulsidas, another celebrated saint of medieval India and a devotee of Rama, laid great emphasis on the practice of Japa. To quote his own words—

सगुन ध्यान रुचि सरस नहिं निर्गुन मन ते दूरि।
तुलसी सुमिरहु रामको नाम सजीवन मूरि॥

"Very hard it is to meditate on God with attributes, what to speak of meditation on God without attributes. So Tulsi says: Always take the name of Rama, and your life will be transformed."

One need not think that this prescription of repeating the sacred word, as a help to develop Bhakti, is arbitrary and without any rational background. In reading a great book one occasionally comes across a passage which is difficult to understand at first; but if one reads it again and again, the meaning suddenly dawns on the mind. In the same way, by repeating the sacred word its deeper significance becomes manifest after a time to the devotee's mind and heart in such a way that he has no longer any doubt about it. It goes without saying that a difficult passage will not yield its meaning, in spite of repetition, if the reader does not give full attention to it. In the same way, the Bhakta who repeats the name of God indifferently or mechanically cannot expect to get the same result as one who does it with deep earnestness and concentration.

These—prayer, holy association, Japa—are after all only preliminary steps in the path of Bhakti-Yoga. The main thing is to acquire Bhakti. Once a devotee gets that, he is safe and his success is assured. If by effort and struggle the main current of a stream is reached, the swimmer will thenceforth be carried along swiftly by the current itself. So long as there is stillness in the air on a hot day, one requires the help of a fan; but as soon as the natural breeze comes there is no more need of this artificial aid. The Bhakta who has developed a genuine love for God can no longer take a false step: he need not, any more, consciously discriminate between right and wrong, nor strive to do the right and reject the wrong. In spite of himself he will move on the right path, because God Himself now holds him by the hand, as it were, and guides him through life. With such a man or woman Bhakti becomes an unerring light, and brings everlasting peace and harmony in the midst of earthly suffering and evil.

Bhakti takes different forms: Some devotees look upon God as Father, some as Mother, some as Child, and so on, till almost every earthly relationship is used according to the devotee's temperament. There are also some who find it impossible to define their exact attitude towards God: to them God is Father as well as Mother; Friend as well as Master. God represents, for such Bhaktas, the combination of all earthly love intensified a hundredfold. When an exceptional devotee develops such intense Bhakti, he has no desire for life, no fear of death. All earthly treasures seem like dross to him and can no longer attract him. Though in the body, he transcends the body-idea. The line of demarcation between life and death, between this world and another, altogether vanishes and has no meaning for him. He knows that, wherever he is, he belongs to God who is omnipresent, omniscient, and omnipotent. If he continues to live, he becomes a blessing to humanity and kindles a light which permanently guides others treading the same path. Even in death he becomes immortal; because he lives on in the hearts of all sincere lovers of God.

KARMA-YOGA

There are some persons who are moved more by the sense of duty than by the necessity of any supplication or prayer to God. They do not wish to see this world in terms of what is to follow after death. To them the present world is real enough and demands one's attention and energy to such an extent that there is no time to indulge in dreams or even in philosophical speculations. They feel they have a duty to themselves, duty to their neighbours, duty to the nation, and, if their heart is expansive enough, duty to the world and humanity. Being of an active temperament—the volitional type—they are always busy with something or other. Hardly have they put one plan into effect, when a hundred others rush into their brains. If they succeed in life, they become great patriots, political leaders, social reformers, philanthropists, scientists, writers, and so on. Their overflowing energy is turned into one or more different channels according to their individual tendencies.

It would be foolish to say that these active workers are outside the domain of God because they do not *formally* worship Him. Many of them are inspired by high idealism, and are honest, sincere, and self-sacrificing. They sometimes possess virtues which any religious man would admire, nay, even long for. From every point of the earth we are equally near to God; and only a narrow-minded fanatic will be able to assert that there is no hope for a person who is outside the fold of an orthodox religion. Every one of our activities is an attempt—often unconscious—to reach Truth or to grasp Reality. If a man of religion sincerely believes that even the footfall of an ant is heard by God, he will not decry those for whom selfless work is the only religion. They may not consciously seek God; but who knows that God might not be seeking them!

There is, however, one difficulty: The power of the human will and the range of human resources are limited. A man cannot always achieve success according to his desire. An Alexander, a Charlemagne, a Napoleon, may be big names in history; but in their personal lives they were failures: they died heartbroken and disappointed. When success came to them in the beginning, they became flushed and elated. Then the Wheel of Fortune turned and failure dogged their steps at every turn. They at last learnt to their cost that in human life even the mightiest have to contend against an Unknown Power which grinds slowly but steadily. They also realised that the human will is not everything and that a time comes when it is humbled to the dust. At first, however, every check to the fulfilment of their desires and ambitions made them angry and unhappy. Every man—good or bad—wants happiness in life. But after struggling for it till the end of his days, he finds that it continually eludes his grasp. The more he struggles for it, the more it recedes; and in the end he realises that the struggle has been all in vain. Napoleon said with a sigh in his declining years that the Empire he had built "was built on sands"!

What, after all, is Duty? This purely human quality (which Wordsworth, in his puritanical zeal, idealised as the "stern daughter of the Voice of God"), proceeds at its best from the social sense; and at its worst, from pride or self-conceit. One cannot remove all the misery from the world. You remove misery in one sphere—if at all you can, it again appears in another sphere. From the dawn of humanity man has been struggling to eliminate suffering from life on this earth; but how far has he succeeded? The answer is given by the continuance, up to our own times, of wars and revolutions involving bloodshed, famine, and pestilence of ever increasing intensity. Our so-called "civilisation" and "culture" appear to be only the thin veneer which conceals the rooted savage in man. It is doubtful whether, in spite of his boast of achievement in the fields of science, art, philosophy, etc., modern man is really happier than his ancestor who lived a thousand years ago. This is not an exaggerated idea born of pessimism, but the simple statement of a stern fact, a hard reality which cannot be ignored, however much we may detest it.

Nevertheless, man must work. He cannot remain, even for a moment, without some kind of work. If he stops outward activities, his inner activities go on all the same. A man may sometimes long intensely to be in solitude, bereft of all work and responsibilities: but how long can he actually stand that condition? It is all a temporary romance which fades away, alas, too soon. It is said that a man who can live happily in solitude for a very long time is either a saint or a beast. The average man, being neither, is just a human being with all the human weaknesses. He must, therefore, work: he cannot shirk duties and responsibilities.

Karma-Yoga teaches man the secret of work: how to work in such a way that, while achieving the maximum result, he will avoid the pangs of disappointment and despair, and at the same time fulfil the spiritual purpose of life. According to this Path of achieving Freedom from bondage, the end of any work should be, not so much the attainment of external success, as a training in unselfishness. If a man wants real happiness, he must needs be unselfish. The more one can sacrifice oneself for the sake of others, the greater is one's joy in life. Although this sounds like a paradox, the truth of it has been proved in countless instances all through the ages. It is very doubtful if you can improve the world; but you can certainly improve yourself by means of unselfish work. Karma-Yoga says: "Work at full speed, with the energy of your whole being; but do not think of the result in terms of success or failure. Avoid being elated at the prospect of success or being oppressed by an anxiety of impending failure: for the sense of success and failure is the outcome of selfishness and egotism—feelings which almost invariably lead to misery. Work like a giant, but be indifferent to the result. If success comes, that is welcome; if the result is failure, that also does not matter. Finally, if you can, work in a spirit of worship—worship of the Divinity in each man, however wretched."

Very few people seem to realise that the person who works whole-heartedly but in a spirit of detachment, accomplishes the task in hand far more efficiently than one who constantly thinks of the result. When a person's sole objective in work is success, the fear of even possible failure worries him so much that he cannot devote his whole energy to the task. One who can be indifferent to success or failure is usually calm and serene; and it is obvious that such a person will work better—especially during a crisis—than one who is always in a feverish anxiety about the result.

One *sure* criterion by which a spiritual life can be judged is unselfishness. The more one grows in spirituality, the more unselfish one becomes. An animal is ordinarily busy only about its own food and comforts. But man thinks about his family, his neighbours, his country. A saint looks on all human beings without any distinction of caste, creed or nationality: the whole world is dear to him, as a manifestation of God. The laws of evolution, in terms of the struggle for existence and the survival of the fittest, are true mainly of the animal kingdom; though even there modern biology has shown the existence of "mutual aid" as an important principle. If a man wants to ascend higher in the scale of spiritual evolution, self-sacrifice and self-effacement are two of the essential steps. Unfortunately, in the West too much emphasis was put during the last century on the theory of the survival of the fittest: with the result that, even today, the average Western man and his Eastern imitator believe they can grow only by elbowing out their neighbours. As a corollary of this, certain nations want to expand by exterminating other nations; and a War-Lord is admired and applauded as a great hero, although he typifies only the baser animal instincts on a magnified scale. In the scale of spiritual values, however, the man who sacrifices himself and forgives others, lives; while he who thinks only of self-aggrandisement perishes. Buddha and Christ, although they have passed into legend, are still names which inspire and transform thousands of lives; but the names of Caesar and Napoleon are of interest only to students of history or psychology as victims of an overreaching ambition for power and conquest.

But what is the causal relation between unselfishness and the realisation of spiritual truths?—it may be pertinently asked. The answer is that it is selfishness that hides Truth from us; that it is egotism that divides man from man and separates him from God. Philosophically speaking, there is only one Existence; but we, in our delusion created by egocentricity, see It as many. Water contained in separate jars may look different in each jar. But if the jars are broken, it will be found that the water is one and the same. Similarly, when a person's egoism and selfishness are destroyed, he becomes one with the Universal Existence.

A Karma-Yogi, therefore, who strives day by day to be more and more unselfish, is, unknowingly, on the path of the highest religion. Without arguing about philosophy, or even spiritual problems, he steadily proceeds towards the realisation of the Supreme Truth. The saying that "the man who keeps his eyes open and works for the world, is more spiritual than the man who shuts his eyes and tells his beads in his cell", may be perfectly true in certain cases. It may be that the man in the cell, if he is not sufficiently alert, will become more and more self-centred; whereas the man who is ready at any moment to sacrifice his all for the sake of others is fast advancing in spiritual growth. When a Karma-Yogi at last succeeds in becoming completely unselfish, Truth will be thrust upon him, even though he did not consciously seek it. When weeds have been entirely removed from the surface of a pond, the water in it will thenceforth reflect the moon, whether that was the object of the weed-clearance or not. In any case, the spiritual significance of a true Karma-Yogi is no less—if not more—than that of a Bhakta who assiduously says his prayers and practises devotions with genuine love.

But one who *works* may not necessarily be devoid of devotional feelings or the spirit of philosophical inquiry. Work can be done in a spirit of Bhakti or with the outlook of a Jnani.

A Karma-Yogi who has deep faith in God will perform his duties as a form of worship. Every work he does is for him an offering to God. The worship which a devotee does in the shrine with flowers and incense, the Karma-Yogi also performs in his own way though out in the broad world and engaged in manifold duties. He acquires almost the same feeling for God and tries to maintain it in every detail of his allotted task. It is said of Brother Lawrence, a Christian Mystic, that he tried at first to feel and afterwards actually felt the presence of God in the course of all the duties—chiefly menial—that he performed at his Monastery throughout the day. The same thing seems to have happened to St. Teresa. Although the Head of a big religious Order, she insisted on doing even household duties like cooking. When asked why she did that, she would reply: "These cooking pots and pans are my instruments of prayer. Through them also I manage to pray." Some workers of the devotional type try to feel that they are only the instruments of God, that their work is meant to carry out the Lord's will. But how is one to know that the performance of a particular task is in furtherance of *God's* Will, and not the selfish will of the doer himself? For an answer to this question, the day-to-day attitude of the worker must be watched and also the effect of the work on his character and conduct of life should be seen. If the Karma-Yogi performs his daily task in a sincere spirit of Bhakti, then he must needs begin to feel that his personal will is gradually giving way to the Divine Will. When this feeling at last ripens into actual experience, he enjoys a calm which nothing in the world can disturb.

Some workers of the devotional type try to see the face of God in every one they meet in life. If they work for their children and family, they think they are serving God in those forms. When they nurse the sick and help the needy, they feel they are worshipping God in those forms, that God has thus come before them to receive their offering. A woman once complained to Sri Ramakrishna that she was so much attached to a child that she could not turn her mind to God. The Paramahamsa consoled her and suggested that she should thenceforth consider the child as an embodiment of God. She followed his advice and soon found that her whole attitude had been transformed, and that her love for the child was now of the same quality as her love for God.

To those workers who have a philosophical bent of mind, the advice of the Gita is that they should remember that they are the Self; that it is the senses which work, impelled by past tendencies and desires; while the Self, which is their inner being, their real existence, is free from all earthly contact, and transcends everything material. The implication of this sublime and pregnant idea is at first caught only by the imagination; but by constantly dwelling on it, while he works, the imagination of the Karma-Yogi will at last give place to experience and he will realise the Self.

It will thus be seen that there are no watertight compartments among the different Yogas. Karma, Bhakti, and Jnana may, and often do commingle with one another in the course of spiritual practice. Only the temperament of the aspirant will determine which of the three is to have a dominant influence in his life.

Persons who are slaves of worldly desires often glibly assert that they are practising Karma-Yoga, in the deluded belief that they work without any personal motive or attachment! They do not realise that the path of a true Karma-Yogi is extremely difficult, and that its success does not depend upon "wishful thinking", however strong. One can deceive others; one can deceive even one's own self; but one cannot deceive God. Success may be obtained in other walks of life through cleverness or make-belief, but certainly not in the spiritual domain. For genuine progress in any spiritual practice—and Karma-Yoga is no exception—one must needs be perfectly sincere; and at the same time alert, introspective, and capable of detecting the thousand and one tricks that the mind is in the habit of playing with each one of us. Recently, a well-known social worker sent a sum of money, collected by her from various persons, to a Relief Committee. She afterwards bitterly complained that, although the names of her donors were given in the Press, there was no mention of the fact that it was *she* who had collected the money from them. It did not seem to occur to her that such a complaint would naturally give rise to the suspicion that her main object in making the collection was to get her name into the newspapers! This is but to cite one concrete instance. Before one can be a true Karma-Yogi, all egoism, even in its most subtle forms, must be stamped out. This requires vigilant care and long practice.

The evil spirit "Mara" tried to tempt even Lord Buddha while he sat in meditation for the realisation of Truth. It tempts also the aspirant who has chosen the path of Karma-Yoga, in various subtle ways. Work, even of the highest type, has got its temptations and intoxications. Some persons plunge themselves into philanthropic and "social service" activities apparently with the idea of reaping a spiritual harvest; but they easily succumb to the desire for name and fame or for material power. It is often found that they work not for the love of God and His children but to feed their own vanity. In their pride and self-conceit they seem to forget that it is not for an insignificant mortal like man to "reform" the world, or to correct the mistakes of God! In their hankering for gratitude they do not realise that if man finds an opportunity for service to any living being, it is *he* who should really thank that being for the privilege to serve. A tree is known by its fruits: When a person busily engaged in philanthropic activities is found to have developed no humility, no compassion—in fact, no distinctive attribute of a spiritual outlook then it is clear that he did not work unselfishly for any spiritual end, but that he worked for some material reward. What is called altruism by such persons is really nothing else but a kind of "alter-egoism" which usually takes the form of some patronising service meant to flatter the worker's ego. In the case of certain Western nations this "alter-egoism" often takes on the familiar name of "the white man's burden" or "trusteeship for the backward races", although its real name is "conquest and exploitation".

Many a budding Karma-Yogi has been

known to have ruined his spiritual progress by collaborating with a leader who, under the guise of religion or reform, was actually engaged in the dangerous game of power-politics. When these unfortunate souls first enter politics, they do so in the sincere hope of doing good to a very large number of people—God's children on earth; but they soon get so deeply entangled in the meshes of power that, in the majority of cases, they find it impossible to extricate themselves. It is such persons who have made Religion hated in certain quarters, as being an ally of the "vested interests" of one sort or another.

Although, in theory, the maxim "work for work's sake" sounds easy, in actual practice very few can follow it unless they have developed, with the grace of God, an extraordinary power of introspection. Without constant awareness and recollection of the ideal, work tends to become a bondage rather than a help. That is why all great spiritual teachers have advised beginners to combine work with prayer and meditation, and to give as little as possible to external action until such time as they are *fit* to act in the right spirit. A Christian mystic has very aptly said: "If we have gone far in orison, we shall give much to action: if we are but middlingly advanced in the inward life, we shall give ourselves only moderately to outward life; if we have only a very little inwardness, we shall give nothing at all to what is external."

To a Westernised Bengali who spoke scornfully of renunciation and emphasised the necessity for educated young men "to resort *only* to such acts as will *uplift* the country", Sri Ramakrishna said, among other things: "Have you seen those tiny crabs that are born in the Ganga just when the rains set in? In this big universe you are even less significant than one of those small creatures. How dare you talk of *helping* the world? ... Let a man get the authority from God and be endowed with His power; then, and then alone, may he think of doing good to others. A man should first be purged of all egotism. Then alone will the Blissful Mother ask him to work for the world." The Master also used to say in similar connections: "Everybody says he is living in the world like King Janaka[1]; but they forget that Janaka had to undergo very hard spiritual practices before he attained success as a great Karma-Yogi. Nowadays, everyone wants to be a Janaka to

[1] An ancient king of India who was a great seer but at the same time held the reins of an important kingdom.

obtain the result without paying the price. Self-deception can go no further!" This Saint's real attitude towards work has been ably summarised by a commentator as follows: "Sri Ramakrishna mistrusted philanthropy that presumed to pose as charity. He warned people against it. He saw in most acts of philanthropy nothing but egoism, vanity, a desire for glory, a barren excitement to kill the boredom of life, or an attempt to soothe a guilty conscience. True charity, he taught, is the result of love of God—service to man in a spirit of worship."

One of the greatest dangers against which an aspirant treading the difficult path of Karma-Yoga must be constantly on guard, is pride, particularly the pride of virtue, resulting in intolerance of the weaknesses of others. Even tolerance, according to Swami Vivekananda is not good enough for a Karma-Yogi; since there is always some element of patronage in one who only tolerates, and patronage invariably means a kind of superiority in the person who gives or helps. If the Karma-Yogi is, therefore, really to serve man "in a spirit of worship", his attitude must be that of total acceptance. Christ had always greater condemnation for the "virtuous" Pharisee who prided himself on his righteousness than for the unfortunate sinner. His utterance: "Judge not, that ye be not judged!" sums up for all time the folly of intolerance. Many a reformer, in his fanatical zeal to save the souls of others, has ended up by becoming, what William Blake called, "a fiend of Righteousness"!

These, then, are some of the main obstacles that beset the path of Karma-Yoga—perhaps the steepest, and the most frequently lost, of the four Paths. This is inevitable, because, whereas the Bhakta, the Jnani, and the Raja-Yogi may often be able to forget the world of man, the Karma-Yogi is constantly required to be "*in* the world, but not *of* it". But there is no need to despair: *provided* the aspirant is—and continues till the end to be—humble, sincere, earnest and persevering, he will in good time, by the grace of God, achieve the same result through unselfish work, that another may obtain by following a different Path.

JNANA-YOGA

Among all the uncertainties of the world the most certain thing is death. The fact that no one can escape death, that death awaits every one as the most inevitable thing in life, has disturbed inquiring minds since the beginning of civilisation, and has roused in them a desire to solve the mystery of existence by searching for the Reality that transcends both life and death. There are of course persons who are either too light-hearted to undertake such a search, or who consider it to be futile. These go on merrily through life, building "castles in the air", making plans and nursing hopes, when suddenly there comes a shock. A beloved friend or relation dies. Where has he gone? No one can say. He was working with such zeal and enthusiasm, with never a thought of death; but all of a sudden he drops down; the curtain falls, and he is to be seen no more on the face of the earth. Such a happening sets even a matter-of-fact man of the world thinking: "Is the world real? If it be real, why does a man suddenly disappear without leaving the slightest trace behind him? And if the call may come at any moment for each one of us to leave the earth, why should we cling so much to our worldly activities? If death be the end of everything, why should we toil so much in life?" Such thoughts may temporarily paralyse one's activities and make him unfit for the world. But is there any doubt that there are good grounds for these disturbing questions?

To the average modern man the question whether the world is real or unreal conveys no meaning. For him there is absolutely no doubt that the world *is* real. He treads the earth, sees the sun and feels the air: how can any doubt arise that these are not real? Even if the shadow of a doubt does arise, it must be immediately suppressed in order that there may be no hampering of his worldly activities. His philosophy of life is: "Have ambitions; have newer and newer forms of desires and employ your best energy to fulfil them. Life is full of conflicts and struggles, which are ingrained in the very nature of things. Face them boldly; and do not spoil your career by too much of analysis or dreaming!"

But this is asking us to see life in a partial aspect only and not to face it in its completeness. Just as an ostrich in danger buries its head under the sand and considers itself safe from pursuing dogs, the unthinking pleasure-seeker deludes himself into the belief that he is perfectly secure in his day-to-day existence in the sense-world. He *dare* not think deeply; because, if he did, the result might be alarming. It is a common experience to be frightened at one's own thoughts. But, however much we may avoid thinking, we cannot escape the stern facts of life and death. The Wheel of Nature turns, and brings before us its unending procession of phenomena, whether we like them or not.

A Jnana-Yogi, however, is not afraid of facing anything in life, or even the spectre of death. He is prepared to see all the aspects of life—pleasant and unpleasant—but, at the same time, he devises means to guard himself against its pitfalls. People glibly say that religious men are afraid of life; but this is far from the truth. Truly religious men are not only not frightened of life, but they also consider death to be only a counterpart of life, and their aim is to go beyond both.

All the activities of man—his desires and ambitions, his hopes and fears—rest on the idea of "I-ness". A man feels: *I* exist; *I* think; *I* desire; and from that feeling starts the wheel of activities of his life. Never for a moment does a man inquire what that "I"

is. If even for five minutes we close our eyes
and try to think about this "I" which is the
basis of all our feverish activities, we get into
a hopeless difficulty: Hands and feet are not
"I"; eyes and ears are not "I"; even the mind
is not "I"—for when we say, *"My* mind",
we at once admit that we are separate from
the mind. Nevertheless, we put so much
faith in and build so many hopes on our "I"
and "Me". One says some angry word and
we get offended; another brings some good
tidings and we feel happy. Modern physics is
no longer sure whether what we see as solid
matter is really material at all; whether, in
he last analysis, "matter" does not reduce
tself to thought, or to some symbol. But
till there is the illusion of the material
vorld before our eyes. In the same way,
hough we do not find any solid basis for
he "I" and "Me", we nevertheless feel all
he time that we exist; and it is on this feel-
ng that the whole citadel of our life rests.

Jnana-Yoga says: "Reject what is false;
nd with a keen sense of discrimination seek
vhat is true." The Jnani, like a valiant
ghter, refuses to identify himself with any-
hing that is unreal. He analyses everything
elonging to the sense-world as "Neti, Neti—
ot this, not this", and, with a sheer effort of

the will, keeps himself unattached to anything that is of a transitory nature. Because he finds on analysis that all earthly desires and relationships possess only a temporary value, he guards himself constantly against the danger of succumbing to their influence. Knowing that his physical body will perish sooner or later, he always tries to kindle in himself the consciousness of his separateness from the body. When a person thus rejects everything that is *not* real, what remains as the residue is the Self or Reality.

Instead of employing straightway the method of rejection, an aspirant following the path of Jnana-Yoga may start with a positive idea, viz that he is the Self as distinguished from the body. In spite of countless failures he repeats to himself this potent idea until one day his "cloud of unknowing" suddenly clears away and in a flash he actually realises that he *is* the Self. At night the stump of a tree is sometimes mistaken for a ghost; but a friend comes along and tells the frightened traveller that it is a tree and not a ghost. The traveller has this idea imprinted upon his mind; and, as he goes near, he finds that what he imagined to be a ghost is in reality nothing but a tree. This illustrates to some extent the process of Jnana-Yoga.

Anyone who attempts to follow this difficult path must be a fearless spirit endowed with almost a superhuman strength of mind. His body must obey his highest thoughts as spontaneously as a supple twig bends at the touch of the wind. But how many can sincerely say that they possess such courage and strength of spirit—rare qualities that, perhaps once in a century, mark out a Swami Vivekananda from his fellows? The average person, with human weaknesses, finds his actions almost always at variance with his ideals and aspirations. Recognising this fact, the Gita says: "Harder is the task for those who aspire after the Unmanifested. Those who have not risen above the body-consciousness will have to suffer if they try to realise the Unmanifested Brahman."

How difficult it is to eliminate the body-idea! You may repeat a thousand times that you are not body but the Spirit; but it requires only a slight headache to draw away all your thoughts again to your perishable body. That is the tragedy of life. The story goes that a patient in a hospital began to repeat the Gita loudly in order to imbibe the idea that he was one with the Eternal Brahman; but as soon as the surgeon came with his knife, the poor man forgot Brahman and began to quake with fear! This is the experience of almost all of us in life.

The Hindu Scriptures therefore enjoin certain preliminary qualifications for those aspiring to practise Jnana-Yoga. The chief of these are a keen sense of discrimination between the Real and the unreal; the absence of a desire for enjoyment of this world or the world to follow; the acquisition of certain powers like control of the mind, control of the senses, the capacity of withdrawing the mind from external objects, the power of physical endurance; supreme faith in one's own power combined with receptiveness to the instructions of the Guru; and, above all, a sincere longing for liberation from the bondage of human existence. No one can deny that these preliminary qualifications, taken together, make an almost impossible demand on the capacity of an average human being. The ordinary mortal is bound to be in despair if he is to be judged by these standards before he is considered fit to practise this form of Yoga. The Scriptures, accordingly, suggest that only those who have been able to master these preliminary disciplines in their past lives would have some hope of success in the path of Jnana-Yoga. However that may be, it is also true that if a man, in spite of his past "Samskaras", sincerely and constantly tries to obtain strength from the source of infinite power that lies hidden within every being, there will at last come a time when the spring of all power and strength will be revealed to him and he will be flooded with a great illumination. Even the weary process of acquiring the preliminary virtues will be automatically hastened if the aspirant honestly tries, from day to day, to live up to the conviction that he is the Eternal Self, and not the perishable body It has been proved by experience that all thoughts—good and bad—have a tremendous influence on one's life. If therefore you always think yourself to be strong, strength will gradually be developed in you, almost without your being aware of it. In the same way, if one can really imagine oneself to be the timeless Self, a subconscious process will be set up by which the weaknesses of the flesh or of the temporal body will gradually vanish. If an aspirant after Jnana-Yoga sincerely follows this method and perseveres in it in spite of repeated failures, he is likely to succeed in the long run. The Scriptures advise that a disciple should know from a Guru who has directly realised the Self the true nature of his being. He should then meditate upon that idea until one day he has himself a direct experience of Reality. This is illustrated by the story that a tiger cub which, happened to be brought up among a flock of sheep, came to believe that it was also a sheep. One day a tiger which fell upon the flock was surprised to find a little tiger living with the sheep. When the cub was told that it was *not* a sheep but a tiger, it refused at first to believe this. Then the tiger took the cub to a pond and showed it its reflection in the water along with his own reflection. This at last convinced the cub that it belonged to the same family as the tiger, and removed its obsession that it was a sheep. In the same way, a disciple with the help of a Guru may come to realise that in reality he is not a bundle of flesh, bones, and blood, but the Eternal Self.

This does not mean that it is easy for an ordinary mortal to act on the belief that he is the Eternal Self. Just as Sri Ramakrishna used to ridicule the claim of some conceited persons that they performed their duties in the spirit of the great Karma-Yogi, King Janaka; so he often exposed the sham of those who pretended they were Jnanis—at one with the deathless Brahman! There are some who dupe themselves into the belief that because, intrinsically, they are the Self, no bad effects

:an follow from any wrongful acts they may :ommit. They console themselves with the dea that since the world is after all a dream —Maya, it matters little what they do. In upport of their thesis they glibly quote the Gita which says that the Self which is deathess does not kill, nor can It be killed. All var, violence and bloodshed may be defended n this basis; but that is equivalent to the 'devil citing the scriptures" for his own purpose! The search for the Eternal Self nvolves a degree of renunciation which no varlord would ever be able to impose on himelf; because if he did, he would suffer unearable agony every time he injured another or his own advancement.

It follows that the hard discipline of Jnana-'oga can be successfully undertaken only by person who is endowed with an exceptionally strong and a keenly analytical mind, Vithout such equipment an aspirant may ither make a mess of his whole spiritual life r, what is worse, develop a false, egoistic hilosophy of the kind described in the foreoing paragraph. It is not enough for the spirant to have only an intellectual conviction that the path of Jnana-Yoga is best suited o his temperament. He must also be preared to fight out his spiritual battle all alone

—in an open field, as it were, and under the open sky. He will have to wrestle constantly with human weaknesses and the subtle tricks which the mind always plays in such cases, and will find no respite from the grim struggle until he reaches a state of mind where he is, to some extent, safe.

It must not however be thought that this Yoga of Knowledge prohibits or spurns aid from any of the other three Yogas. A budding Jnani need not eliminate all elements of Bhakti from his life. He may actually invoke strength by prayer to God and devotion to his Guru. When, in the beginning, the aspirant longs for light and finds nothing but darkness before him, the help and blessing of a Guru may be his only source of strength and hope. Similarly, unselfish work of some kind, undertaken in the spirit of a Karma-Yogi, may often be a useful preliminary to the practice of Jnana-Yoga. In the very nature of things it is well-nigh impossible for an average person to embark straightway on the arduous path of Jnana-Yoga. He has hundreds of desires and innumerable forms of attachment to pull him back from the straight and narrow course; and it would be foolish to expect him, all at once, to crush such desires or to become completely detached

By engaging himself in some form of activity in the service of his fellow-beings and by cultivating non-attachment, he may gradually rise above desires and attain the degree of Self-purification necessary for the practice of Jnana-Yoga. The greater the self-purification one can achieve, the fitter one will be for the exacting demands of the Yoga of Knowledge. Again, strict control of the mind and a high degree of concentration are essential for the practice of Jnana-Yoga, and these can best be acquired by the methods prescribed by Raja-Yoga.

A sceptic may well ask: "Can any man born of the womb of a woman actually realise that he is a bodiless spirit—the Eternal Self? Does not the very idea sound impossible and fantastic? Has any human being ever experienced that condition; and if so, does history bear testimony to such an experience?" Yes, history does testify, in more than one case, that such a state has come within the domain of human experience. It is said that when Alexander invaded India, he came across an old sage whom he wanted to take with him to Greece. But as the wise man refused to accompany the great conqueror, Alexander at first entreated and cajoled him, and at last threatened to take his life if he persisted in his stubbornness. At this the wise man burst out into a fit of loud laughter and said: "I have never heard a greater lie than that. For you can never kill me who am birthless, deathless, and ever-existent." This incident has passed into history and can be found in Greek accounts. Nearer home, and at a later period, the great saint Sankaracharya also realised that unity with the Ultimate Reality which is the final goal of the Yoga of Knowledge, as of the other three Yogas. This philosopher-saint's writings bear ample evidence to the fact of such a realisation. Therein, he has analysed and described in great detail the state of superconsciousness of the person who experiences this unitive knowledge of God. It is also beyond doubt that some of Sankara's disciples similarly experienced the truth of his philosophy in actual life. Thus Sankara and other great Jnanis have not only proved by philosophical reasoning that there is only one Existence on which human ignorance weaves the dream of manifoldness, but have also unmistakably shown that the fact of such an Existence, outside the ambit of time and space, can actually be experienced by a human being possessing the requisite spiritual insight and power.

This experience of the timeless, spaceless Reality must necessarily be beyond thought and speech; for, when there is only the One, who will speak or think about whom? The person who has actually experienced such a state can, after coming down to the normal plane, only vouch for the fact of that experience; but it would not be possible for him to describe, within the limitations of time and space which are now imposed on him, *what* it actually was. Superficially, the highest state experienced by a Jnani may be compared to the condition of deep sleep: because when the sleeper awakes, he also cannot describe that condition except as one of complete forgetfulness of the universe. There is, however, a great difference between the two conditions; inasmuch as the man who has realised the Ultimate Truth is so transformed by his experience that his every word and action thereafter bespeaks the highest wisdom and spiritual insight. A fool goes into deep sleep and comes back a fool; but when a Jnani ascends to the highest state of knowledge, he comes down—if at all he can do so—armed with a vision that is of supreme value to humanity.

It has often been asked whether a man can survive the state during which he realises that he is the Eternal Spirit, and *not* the body or the mind. When a person has transcended the body-idea, it naturally follows that the body will fall off; and it has been recorded that, ordinarily, a Jnani, after realising the Supreme Reality, does not long survive that tremendous experience. There are, however, exceptional beings, like Sankara, who even after the supreme realisation retain the noble desire to teach humanity the means of attaining such a state. These souls voluntarily sacrifice the eternal freedom from bondage, which they have attained, in order to bring salvation to others. To them the portals of the highest experience remain for ever open; but they refuse to enter those gates until they can take along with them some at least of those who, suffering and heavy-laden, struggle hard for light and illumination. These are the great prophets, seers, and mystics who keep the torch of the spirit burning when infinite darkness threatens to envelop humanity. It is they who by simply living arrest, at least for a time, the headlong descent of a weary world into the abyss of ignorance. They are the representatives of God on earth.

RAJA-YOGA

In non-philosophical language, Raja-Yoga is the science and art of concentrating the mind. A mind which lacks one-pointedness or concentration can never be a fit instrument for the realisation of Truth. At moments when a man's mind is perfectly calm and still, the Truth some time suddenly dawns on him even though he has not consciously sought for it. When there is no movement of the waters in a lake, when no waves or ripples disturb the surface, the moon is clearly reflected. In the same way, when the mind is not agitated by distractions or wandering thoughts (which have been compared by contemplatives "to dust, to swarms of flies, to the movements of a monkey stung by a scorpion"), it is possible for it to glimpse the Truth. It is said that if one can achieve perfect concentration of the mind even for a few minutes, the highest Truth will be his. But how difficult is such an achievement! The mind's tendency is always to wander, to roam over heaven and earth, to take the past and future in its sweep. And the more you try to control it by mere force of will, the more unruly it becomes. From the depths of the subconscious rise thoughts which are sometimes frightening to look at. One feels tired, distressed, and disheartened at the seeming futility of the struggle. Patanjali, who first spoke of Raja-Yoga, analyses most minutely the nature and workings of the mind and suggests ways and means of bringing it under control and making it calm. Yoga, according to him, is the method of stopping the modifications of the mind-stuff. Just as the surface of a lake undergoes modifications, in the shape of waves and ripples, when lashed by the wind and therefore cannot reflect the moon, in the same way our wandering thoughts which blot out the vision of Truth are modifications of the mind-stuff, resulting from reactions to various experiences—past and present—in life. Raja-Yoga teaches the method of preventing the mind from undergoing unnecessary modifications and giving vent to purposeless thoughts.

The practice of Raja-Yoga actually consists of eight stages—Yama, Niyama, Asana, Pranayama, Pratyahara, Dharana, Dhyana, and Samadhi. But strangely enough, just as many persons are inclined to think that the only Yoga is Raja-Yoga, so others like to believe that Raja-Yoga consists mainly in the practice of Pranayama. Pranayama is the name given to various breathing exercises which are meant to help and ensure concentration. Since rhythmic breathing has usually been found to be an accompaniment of the mind approaching concentration, it follows that ill-regulated breathing would be a hindrance in the struggle to acquire one-pointedness. An aspirant in the path of Raja-Yoga is therefore generally advised to practise some form of Pranayama *along with* one or more of the seven other disciplines mentioned above. But perhaps because of the novelty of the thing and the popular belief that its practice leads to the acquisition of supernatural powers, Pranayama has been given undue importance by the mystery-mongers. The fact is that Pranayama is only *one* of the methods—and that also an indirect method—of acquiring concentration. Even so, without the personal guidance of an experienced teacher, it is a method which is dangerous for one's health, whereas there are others which are equally helpful but not so unsafe. Many a person who, in an enthusiasm to practise Yoga as something strange and mysterious, has done Pranayama to excess without expert guidance, has ended by becoming a physical and mental wreck.

Of all the Yogas, Raja-Yoga has been the most abused. The mind is a storehouse of infinite powers; and as it begins to concentrate, one sometimes experiences strange psychic phenomena. Ignorant and foolish persons—generally insincere and not really earnest about the goal of realising the Supreme Truth—make too much of these psychic phenomena, and more often than not, turn their experiences to material ends. By means of concentration the mind may become such a fine instrument that its possessor may at times develop certain supernormal powers like that of seeing into the future, or reading another's thoughts. Although such powers in themselves have hardly any spiritual value, the person who has acquired them may easily succumb to the temptation of making a business out of them. On the other hand, a dishonest person might only pretend to have those powers and deceive those who are unwary or credulous. It is for this reason that, in the eyes of many, Yoga has become synonymous with magic, charlatanry, deception, and imposture. Those who exhibit tricks like eating nails, swallowing poisonous chemicals, burying themselves under the earth and still remaining alive, are applauded as great Yogis, and draw to themselves crowds of mystery-mongers, especially persons who want to satisfy the morbid curiosity of their own diseased minds. Unfortunately, many a casual visitor to India from the West first shows unusual interest in these tricks of the pseudo-Yogis and then writes about them a sensational book which can only have the effect of making India and Indian religion look ridiculous. The only consolation is that virtue and vice, honesty and dishonesty, always exist side by side in this world; and that truthfulness and a genuine search for Reality are not the monopoly of any particular nation or country. Cheats and rogues stalk the earth to seize upon fools as their victims; but, for God's sake, do not call these pretenders "Yogis" or "Mahatmas", and afterwards, when duped, blame India and its religion!

An abnormal interest in psychic phenomena or in the display of certain powers or *siddhis* has been characteristic not only of the ignorant and credulous but sometimes also of the highly intellectual, particularly in Christian countries. This is one of the paradoxes of spiritual life which Aldous Huxley's sensitive perception has succeeded in unravelling in his great book *Grey Eminence*:

"... orthodox Christianity has always tended to overvalue supernormal occurrences, to identify the unusual with the divine, to confound the merely psychic with the spiritual. This worship of the odd is a phenomenon observable on two levels, the primitive and the highly intellectual—on the level of simple credulous people like Louis XIII and the average peasant and on the level of scientists impressed by the evidence of things that cannot be explained in terms of the current hypotheses; of a Pascal, for example, arguing from miracles to the truth of Christian theology; of a Descartes dallying in his youth with Rosicrucianism; of an Oliver Lodge building a religion on the foundation of evidence suggesting the survival, after death, of a certain psychic factor; of a Carrel impressed by supernormal healing and the power of prayer. Trained as they are to concentrate upon the events of the world of space and time, men of science are peculiarly liable, when they turn religious, to revert to that primitive kind of religion in which 'miracles' play an important part. They are concerned less with the 'kingdom of heaven within' than with external 'signs', less with the knowledge of eternity than with power in space-time. Their religion, in a word, is not mystical, but a kind of occultism."

Genuine spiritual life of any kind whatever

always rests on the cultivation and practice of ethical virtues. One cannot make any real spiritual progress so long as the character has not been firmly built. Light and darkness cannot coexist at the same time. If an aspirant who has chosen one or more of the four great Paths of Yoga, wishes to make genuine progress towards realising the Supreme Truth, it is essential that his daily conduct and dealings in the ordinary, even trivial, affairs of life should conform to his spiritual practices. 'Many of those", says Aldous Huxley, "who undertake spiritual exercises, whether Yogic or Christian, tend all too frequently to confine their efforts at concentrating the mind strictly to business hours—that is to say, to the hours they actually spend in meditation. They forget that it is possible for a man or woman to achieve, during meditation, a high degree of mental concentration, and even a kind of subjectively satisfying pseudo-ecstasy, while remaining at bottom an unregenerate ego. It is not an uncommon thing to meet with people who spend hours of each day doing spiritual exercises and who, in the intervals, display as much spite, prejudice, jealousy, greed and silliness as the most 'unspiritual' of their neighbours. The reason for this is that such people make no effort to adapt to the exigencies of ordinary life those practices which they make use of during their times of formal meditation. This is, of course, not at all surprising. It is much easier to catch a glimpse of reality under the perfect conditions of formal meditation than to 'practise the presence of God' in the midst of the boredoms, annoyances and constant temptations of family and professional life. What the English mystic, Benet Fitch, calls 'active annihilation' or the sinking of the self in God at every moment of the day, is much harder to achieve than 'passive annihilation' in mental prayer. The difference between the two forms of self-annihilation is analogous to the difference between scientific work under laboratory conditions and scientific work in the field. As every scientist knows, a great gulf separates the achievement of results in the laboratory and the application of one's discoveries to the untidy and disconcerting world outside its walls. Laboratory work and work in the field are equally necessary in science. Analogously, in the practice of the unitive life, the laboratory work of formal meditation must be supplemented by what may be called 'applied mysticism' during the hours of everyday activity."

Raja-Yoga, therefore, puts great emphasis
n the ethical life. The very first stage in
he practice of this Yoga—Yama—deals with
he mastery of certain important virtues.

Yama is the collective name given to the
ractice of five great virtues, namely, non-
njury (or love), truthfulness, non-covetous-
ess, continence, and non-receiving of gifts.

It is found, in the ultimate analysis, that
he mind is restless because we react too
uickly and intolerantly to external circum-
tances. A man utters some angry words, and
t once we get excited and upset. We return
ngry words, we get rattled and become un-
alanced. Such persons can never expect to
ake rapid progress towards the realisation
f Truth, even if it were possible for them to
ave calmness of mind in times of meditation.
o Patanjali asks us to practise *non-injury* or
ve. If a person can bring himself to have
enuine love for one and all—even for a
rmer enemy—he is no longer in danger of
sing his peace of mind. The man who is
l-loving and all-forgiving is naturally calm
nd quiet. Being always at peace with him-
lf, he not only finds it easy to concentrate
is mind during the hours of meditation, but
so carries peace with him wherever he is
uring the rest of the waking day.

The effect of practising *truth* in thought word, and deed is no less beneficial to spirit ual progress. The truthful man can alway afford to be frank and fearless, because he ha nothing to hide and has no need to burder or disturb his mind with any subterfuge. B continued practice, it is possible for one t develop such an intense faith in truth tha it finally becomes easy for him to face lif calmly in almost any situation, howeve strange or difficult. Life becomes unnecessaril complex for us, because we try either to hid or to twist truth, because we are accustome to circumlocution. In the effort to keep u the pretence of being truthful, we waste great deal of useful mental energy and mak our journey on this earth more difficult tha it need be. A person who is perfectly hone with himself and with others finds life, o the whole, simple and is able to keep h thoughts on a higher plane much longe than another who is secretive, or who m noeuvres for success.

The man who has practised *non-covetou ness* is not disturbed by worldly desire Intrinsically, man's needs are very few; b there is always a tendency to create artifici wants. Man hankers after more and mo until all his energy is spent in the fulfilme of those wants and he has no time left for any higher thinking.

Continence is another virtue which is essential for the practice of any form of Yoga. The man who is chaste in thought, word, and deed is free from many of the troubles which a slave of passion brings upon himself. His continent habits enable him to store an amount of mental energy which can be easily diverted to the building up of his higher life. A common method employed by spiritual aspirants, throughout the ages, for overcoming their passions has been the infliction of various forms of austerities on the body which the all-loving St. Francis of Assisi used to call "Brother Ass". The Body undoubtedly exerts considerable influence over he mind; but, as all the great mystics were not slow to realise, mortification, however igorous, of the body alone is not sufficient to bring the mind under control. On the contrary, a healthy body is generally a prerequisite for a healthy mind. Only the man who as come to know, even partially, his divine ature and whose mind, as a result of such nowledge, has undergone complete transformation can be perfectly chaste in thought, word, and deed. Others will have to struggle and be on their guard against the passions until they acquire such knowledge in the fulness of time. One thing is certain—that in the practice of any difficult virtue like continence, as in life itself, it is always better to emphasise positive thoughts in preference to negative ideas. "If you go towards the East", as Sri Ramakrishna used to say, "you are so much farther from the West". The more one acquires genuine love for God or Truth, the safer is one from the influx of base thoughts. That is an inescapable law of the mind which the psycho-analyst calls "sublimation".

Anyone who aspires to be a Yogi must be very careful in the matter of *receiving gift* from others. There are very few persons in the world who are really unselfish. If, therefore, a person gives something to another there is generally in the mind (most often the subconscious mind) of that giver som selfish thought or motive that is bound t have an untoward effect, however remote, o the mind of the person who receives; for al mind is one. Unless, as rarely happens, th gift has absolutely no motive behind it and i rendered in a spirit of worship, there cannc but be some falling off—however slight—i the integrity of the recipient. An aspirar in any of the Paths of Yoga must therefore always guard himself against an indiscriminate acceptance of gifts.

The second stage of Raja-Yoga—Niyama—consists of the practice of cleanliness, contentment, austerity, studying the Scriptures, and self-surrender to God.

Cleanliness refers to purity of the body as well as of the mind. *Contentment* means a cheerful acceptance of life accompanied by an elimination of worldly desires; but it does not exclude the hankering for spiritual progress. Some amount of *austerity* is necessary for the aspirant. Living in luxury and enjoying all the comforts of life, one cannot attain success in Yoga. On the other hand, too much of austerity is also bad because it undermines the health. A genuine aspirant after the goal of Yoga has nothing to do with those who perform austerities for their own sake, either to get the approbation of an ignorant public or for the inner satisfaction of having done something unusually strange and difficult. The *study of the Scriptures,* to be of any use, must be thorough and discriminating: while *self-surrender to God* must naturally be accompanied by a love for Him which asks for no return.

It will be seen that all the practices described under the heads Yama and Niyama are highly conducive to mental peace and calm. One who has succeeded in mastering them will therefore not only acquire easily the power of concentration, but, what is more, make his mind a fit instrument for contact with Reality.

The third stage of Raja-Yoga is the practice of Asanas or postures. A posture in which one can sit for a long time with ease and without any discomfort is essential for the practice of meditation. If the body (particularly the legs) has to be constantly changed from one position to another, the mind cannot be concentrated. The necessity of mastering a suitable Asana is to ensure that, while meditating, the thoughts are not brought down to the body-consciousness because of physical discomfort. As in the case of Pranayama, too much has been made of Asanas also by the sensation-mongers. Any simple and convenient posture is good enough for practising meditation; but persons calling themselves great Yogis often impose upon the unwary public by showing off difficult feats of Asana which have nothing to do with spiritual development. Some practise Asanas as a substitute for physical exercise. There is no ıarm in doing this provided such persons do ıot pretend to be Yogis.

Mention has already been made of ranayama, the fouth stage of Raja-Yoga. \s explained, it is the name given to certain ›reathing exercises, performed to the accom›animent of a sacred word, as a help to :oncentration. It may be repeated that an .spirant's mind may come to serious harm if ıe performs these exercises indiscriminately vithout the guidance of an expert teacher.

Pratyahara, the fifth stage of Raja-Yoga, s the method by which the senses may be 'estrained from running after their respecive sense objects. For example, the eyes gaze vith delight or aversion at various objects, .nd carry impressions to the mind which, later ›n, cause some kind of disturbance. The ›ther senses like taste, hearing, touch, and mell repeat, either singly or together, the ame story in varying degrees. If, therefore, ve can control the senses and somehow pre'ent them from receiving undesirable impresions, many a trouble can be checked at its 'ery source. The method which would :nable a person to do this is bound to be of he utmost value to any spiritual aspirant.

Dharana, Dhyana, and Samadhi are the 'emaining three stages of Raja-Yoga. They

are also succeeding stages in the practice c
meditation, which is an indispensable elemer
of all the Yogas. Through the successfu
practice of Dharana and Dhyana, the aspi
ant can achieve so much concentration tha
he at last becomes fit to immerse himself int
Samadhi, which is nothing else but divin
down to the inmost Self and realising Truth

In order to practise meditation, every aspir
ant requires, at least in the beginning, som
concrete objects on which to meditate
Technically, Yoga has been defined as "a
method of stopping the mind-stuff from
acquiring modifications". According to
Patanjali, the most effective way of doing
this is to concentrate the "mind-stuff" by
meditation on God. On the assumption
(based on authentic experience) that the
sound-symbol of God is the sacred word
"Om", the aspirant is asked to repeat this
word at time of meditation, as also when doing Pranayama.

Raja-Yoga (the *Royal* Path of Union) is
probably the most scientific and practical of
all the four Yogas. The profound knowledge
of the mind, including its subconscious depths
and its superconscious heights, on which
Patanjali has based his teaching, might make
any modern psychologist green with envy!

This Yoga does not ask us to take anything for granted. It does not talk of "Grace" or of "The Chosen Few". It simply says that whoever sincerely follows the instructions will get at least some results—more or less, according to his capacity—and that these results will fortify his belief and encourage him to proceed further. It goes without saying that, as in the case of all other practices, quick results can be achieved only by those who are most energetic.

The reader must have noticed that the practices enjoined by Raja-Yoga form an indispensable basis for a successful pursuit of the other Yoga Paths, especially Bhakti-Yoga and Jnana-Yoga. Neither the Bhakta nor the Jnani can ever dispense with the practice of Dhyana, or meditation, in one form or another; and this in turn suggests the practice of Asana, Pratyahara, Dharana, etc., as also the cultivation of the ethical virtue enumerated by Patanjali. As a matter of fact, the points of difference between these three Yogas are only technical or philosophical and of interest mainly to scholars and dialecticians. The sincere aspirant, hungering for the realisation of Truth, will never care to notice these differences. In his great longing for the knowledge of Reality, he will try to get help and illumination from wherever he can.

Hinduism possesses this noteworthy characteristic, that it not only recognises all religions to be true, but also gives, *within* a particular religion, absolute freedom of choice and scope to every individual, according to his temperament. In actual fact, these Yogas deal not so much with religions as with individuals: each individual being given the option to follow the Path he likes best. Moreover, the four great Paths of Love, Work, Knowledge, and Mind-control form the fundamental basis (with slight variations, here and there, according to time and circumstances) of all religions; and any man or woman belonging to one of them, or even to *none* at all, is free to follow one or more of the chosen avenues of Truth.

LAST WORDS

It is, on the whole, an easy matter to describe Yoga in terms of the intellect, or to discuss it in philosophical language. Being however the essence of all religions, Yoga, for its true understanding, depends not on words but on experience. Although a person can finish reading a map of the world in ten minutes, it will probably take him ten lives actually to visit all the places he has seen on that map. So, it is said that perhaps only one in a million has the good fortune to attain complete success in Yoga: the others will have to rest content only with the joy of struggling for the Ideal, or at best with just a partial, flitting glimpse of Reality. This naturally disheartens many and scares away others. Some are even led to think of Yoga as a wild-goose chase: because, while we see and know of many successful men in all walks of life, in the field of Yoga we rarely come across one who can say—unless he is a cheat or a victim of self-deception—that he has actually reached the destination. It is perhaps once in a thousand years that a prophet or seer is born who can talk with authority on the essence of religion, and even the voice of such a one is soon drowned in the confusion that always rages in the world.

One thing however is certain: If the path is recognised to be right and the goal to be worthy of attainment, there is no alternative left for the determined and sincere pilgrim but to struggle on and on, even though "the road winds uphill all the way, yea, to the very end"! Hundreds may fail to reach the ultimate goal and thousands may succumb halfway on the journey; but the struggle, once begun, cannot be given up unless the traveller is prepared to be called a coward. In every undertaking there is the fear or risk of failure; but that never deters any brave heart from doing his chosen task, however difficult. After all, are not "the glorious failures" of history far more lovable and worthy of emulation than those who have achieved success in ignoble pursuits? The words "Nothing fails like success"—paradoxical though they seem—apply so often to some worldly achievement gained at the expense of the degradation of the soul!

Vedanta gives the reason why an average man—the Old Adam—finds the struggle to reach God so hard. It is the law of Karma, the result of actions performed in past lives, that does not allow one to progress as quickly as one would like to. But Vedanta also says that a person can largely determine the future by his present activities; which means that each individual has sufficient freedom to wipe off, to a great extent, the bad effects of his past Karma by means of good action in this life. "Trailing clouds of glory, do we come from God who is our home", and to God we ultimately return; but the time required for the return may be long or short, according to the degree of one's readiness and earnestness. An intense spiritual struggle means an attempt to squeeze the good thoughts and acts of perhaps a thousand lives into one. The struggle becomes mighty—almost pathetically grand—when a bold aspirant resolves to complete in a single life what it would take others many, many lives to achieve.

And, after all, what does it matter even if the bravest of aspirants does not fully succeed in achieving the intended result, in spite of the intensity of his struggle? It is far better to have struggled and lost, than not to have struggle at all. Moreover, it is an incontrovertible law of nature that no labour is lost, no sincere attempt goes in vain. According to the Gita, Arjuna asked Sri Krishna:

"What happens to the man who, sincerely following the path of Yoga, breaks down halfway? Losing this world and the next, is he destroyed like clouds scattered by the wind?"

To this the Lord replied:

न हि कल्याणकृत्कश्चिद्द् दुर्गतिं तात गच्छति ।

—"A doer of good can never come to grief, my child. No harm can betide him here or hereafter."

The Scriptures say that an aspirant who has failed to achieve success in Yoga in one life is born again, and continues the work left unfinished, with greater advantages than before.

So none need despair.

BOOKS ON YOGA
BY SWAMI VIVEKANANDA

Raja-Yoga explains the union of the individual soul with the universal soul through the 'control of the modifications of the mind'.

Pages 306 Rs. 35.00

Six Lessons on Raja-Yoga

Pages 32 Rs. 7.00

Bhakti-Yoga deals with the methods of realizing the Lord through divine love, unassociated with mundane cravings.

Pages 116 Rs. 16.00

Karma-Yoga tells how the individual soul realizes its oneness with the universal soul by doing one's duty without attachment to the fruits thereof.

Pages 138 Rs. 16.00

Jnana-Yoga discusses the way of realization of truth through discrimination that Brahman alone is real and all else is illusory.

Pages 421 Rs. 40.00

Prabuddha Bharata

or Awakened India

An English Monthly Organ of the Ramakrishna Order started by Swami Vivekananda in 1896

Conducted by the monks of the Ramakrishna Order at Advaita Ashrama, P.O. Mayavati, Dt. Champawat, 262524 Uttaranchal, and published from 5 Dehi Entally Road, Kolkata 700014, it is dedicated to the propagation of Universal Religion, Comparative Philosophy, Education, Art, and other topics of international interest.

Annual Subscription:

India & Nepal	Rs. 80
Sri Lanka & Bangladesh	Rs. 180
U.S.A. & Canada (Air Mail)	US$ 25
Other Countries (Air Mail)	UK£ 18
European Union	€ 23

The wavy waters in the picture are symbolic of Karma; the lotus, of Bhakti; and the rising-sun, of Jnana. The encircling serpent is indicative of Yoga and the awakened Kundalini Shakti, while the swan in the picture stands for the Paramatman (Supreme Self). Therefore the idea of the picture is that by the union of Karma, Jnana, Bhakti, and Yoga, the vision of the Paramatman is obtained.

—SWAMI VIVEKANANDA

ISBN 81-7505-048-9

Rs.12